"NOT JUST FOR CHRISTMAS...."

An anthology of short stories, verses and playlets

By Carol Reeve

An environmentally friendly book printed and bound in England by
www.printondemand-worldwide.com

This book is made entirely of chain-of-custody materials

www.fast-print.net/store.php

NOT JUST FOR CHRISTMAS...
An anthology of short stories, verses and playlets

A catalogue record for this book is available from the British Library

ISBN 978-178456-105-5

First Published 2014 by
Fast-Print Publishing of Peterborough, England.

Contents:

"Not just for Christmas..."

Short Stories

Playlets

Verses

Foreword

"A dog is for life, NOT JUST FOR CHRISTMAS….."

This anthology is dedicated with love to my grandchildren and their parents.

Young people especially will enjoy my stories and verses about the various pets that have shared my life, also lonely dragons, imaginary children, and my own interpretation of various historical events, such as King Canute shouting at the sea.

The playlets can be read aloud or acted in drama class. Many of the verses were inspired just by their title, such as The Vending Machine and Cold Hands.

I hope this anthology will encourage young people not only to read, but to write and to act, and always to take notice of the world around them with respect and affection.

Carol Reeve

Not Just For Christmas

1) Christopher. The Golden Retriever 1931.

Christopher lay on the grass, eyes closed, apparently asleep, but his ears were listening. The leaves overhead moved gently in the afternoon breeze, watched by the little girl lying in the big pram beside him. Suddenly she let out a sob, followed by another, but Christopher had already leapt to his four feet and was running up the garden path and into the house.

He found Nanny in the kitchen. Standing in front of her, his tail at half-mast, his ears pricked and his eyes shining up at her, his whole body spoke for him.

Christopher

“Oh dear” she said, “Is the baby crying? Come on, let’s go and see what’s the matter.” Together they went out into the garden, Christopher leading the way, constantly turning back to make sure she was following before rushing on again.

The little child looked up, her face covered with tears, and smiled at her Nanny. Christopher peeped over the edge of the pram, and a small hand reached across to pat his head.

In the months to come, he would remain her constant guardian and companion, standing firm as she gripped his tail and tried to crawl. Later, he let her hold tight to his fur coat or collar when she finally managed to stand up beside him.

He never strayed far from the pushchair during their outings to the Park, and one of her first words was "Kiss-fer!".

Best of all, he allowed her to share his big kennel out in the yard by the garage, and they would snuggle together in the warm straw while Nanny shouted their names in vain.

He was my first dog, my first love, and my very best friend during all the eight years of his life.

2. Peggy. The Border Terrier. 1939

I was eight years old when Peggy arrived. My father explained that this small, excitable little puppy now belonged to me, and I would be responsible for taking her for walks, feeding her, and teaching her to be house-trained. That was the most difficult part, but I explained to Peggy that dogs had to go to the toilet out in the garden, not all over the carpets indoors which caused Doris the maid to be rather unkind. Peggy soon learnt to yap when she needed to spend a penny, or even twopence, and I would follow her around the garden with a little trowel.

Peggy was even allowed to sleep upstairs in my bedroom, in her own basket, but she much preferred lying on the eiderdown close to her young mistress. We did not tell anyone, of course.

Peggy

As Peggy grew up, she became extremely attractive to the young hounds in the village, which assembled on the tennis court and had to be chased away by Wisbech, the gardener. Unfortunately, Peggy fell in love with one of her admirers, and it soon became noticeable that she was going to have puppies.

My father took Peggy away in the car to her original kennels, "for her confinement" he said – well, he was a doctor so he knew about such things. But alas, Peggy did not return home, and I was never told what had happened to her.

I presumed that I was being punished for saying or doing something really terrible, and now I had no-one to talk to, to cuddle or to love.

Then Skeet came to my rescue.

3. Skeet. The Golden Labrador. 1940

Skeet was a big golden Labrador, a gun dog used to chasing the rabbits that nibbled the vegetation on the farm where he lived. It was the first year of World War Two, and Skeet's master had just been called up to join the Army. He mentioned this to his doctor, my father, adding that his dog would be in need of a new home. Within days, my father and I drove the two miles to the farm to meet him. Skeet leapt all over me, washing my face with his rough tongue and whirling his tail round in circles. There was no doubt – Skeet wanted to live with us.

He had always slept in a stable on the farm, so that first night he was tied up to Christopher's old kennel. He howled. And he howled. And he HOWLED.....

Exasperated, my father stomped outside intending to admonish the dog. He returned a few minutes later with Skeet at his heels. The dog made straight for the rug in front of the living room fire, grinned at everyone, stretched out full length and fell asleep.

The following morning, Skeet was let out to "spend a penny". Ten minutes later he had not reappeared, so we all went out into the garden and called him.

No reply. He had disappeared. There was no sign of him anywhere. I was distraught.

Hours later, at dusk, we heard an urgent whine outside the kitchen, then an impatient scratching at the door. I ran to open it.... Skeet was damp and bedraggled. He went straight to his water bowl and drank deeply. We were told later that the local policeman had seen Skeet loping down the lane to his old home. He must have searched all around the farm, but once he was quite sure that the place was deserted, he had decided to come back to his new, loving family.

He spent the war years with us, but never returned to his original home. He passed away just as the war ended, so Wisbech and my father wrapped him in a blanket, laid him in the dug-out shelter, then filled it all in. They sowed grass seed on the mound, and planted daffodil bulbs ready to welcome Spring and a new year.

4) Singhy The Dalmatian 1945

The end of the War meant the start of a new life for me – at Boarding School many miles away from home. I came back for the holidays, of course, and one summer my father took me for a surprise visit to some very posh kennels in the next village. The lady owner specialised in breeding Dalmatian dogs, and she had proudly invited the doctor to come and see the recent arrivals.

There were seven, fat little squirming puppies, just a few weeks old, in a pen with their mother. Their faces were wrinkled and their noses were pink, and I wanted to keep them all, but my father said "Just pick one, darling."

It was very hard to choose, but there was one particularly sweet puppy who looked up at me and seemed to be saying "Here I am -I'm the one!"

A few weeks later, we went to fetch him, and carried him into his new home.

"We must think of a name for him". That was difficult – he had a pedigree name already, the Maharajah of somewhere, so it ought to be an Indian sort of name.

We finally settled on Singhy, with a "j" sound, and he soon answered to it. As he grew, so did his spots – just a few at first, but soon his white coat was covered with patches of black spots, all over his body even his tail, with black ears and a black nose.

One summer holiday, we all went to Cornwall, with our cousins, where one evening Singhy chased a rabbit on the grassy slope high above the sea coves. But they both disappeared quite suddenly and we realised that the dog must have fallen down the side of the cliff, and into the swirling sea. We watched in horror as he struggled against the waves and finally managed to climb out onto an overhanging rock. He could climb no further, and looked up at us in terror. Cousin Hugh was very brave: he began to climb down the cliff and eventually reached the frightened dog, grabbed his collar and began to drag him back up to his waiting family. We carried him back to our holiday home, and sent for a local vet. Singhy was exhausted, but no bones were broken, so the next day it was agreed to take him home to recuperate. He lay across my lap and my mother's in the back seat of the car, and slept as we stroked him. He was thoroughly spoilt for days after his adventure, but he was never allowed to chase rabbits again.

At a Charity Fair people were asked to guess how many spots he had. No-one got it right – I knew, I had counted them already – there were 513.

When my parents divorced, my mother went to live in the town, and took Singhy with her. My father insisted that the dog was his and should be returned, but she refused. Angrily he took her to court. The local policeman gave evidence:

"That dog used to escape and chase the cattle in nearby fields. When I rang the doctor to tell him to keep the dog under control, he'd say 'He's not my responsibility - he's my wife's. You tell her.' " So Singhy stayed with my mother and spent the rest of his life being spoilt by her and her household of foreign students.

5. Ferrari The Boxer 1960

Brian and I were married in May 1957, and our first home was a small rented flat in York. But when we later moved to Bradford and bought a semi-detached house with a garden, close to open fields, we talked about finding a dog. But with both of us working in the town six days a week, it could be difficult. However, my mother was having her hair done at the hairdressers, when she overheard the lady in the next cubicle saying: "It's such a shame, Ferrari is a beautiful boxer dog, but he needs a new home and nobody seems to want him!" Mrs Gilbert called out "Excuse me, but I think my daughter would love to have him!"

Apparently Ferrari had had his nose put out of joint by the arrival of a new pet, a noisy unhousetrained baby. One of them had to go.....

Names and addresses were exchanged, the problem of transporting the dog was discussed and agreed, and a week later Brian and I went down to Exchange Station, Bradford, to meet the train from Cambridge, and walked the length of the train to the guards van at the end. Ferrari was inside, with a label on his collar – "THIS DOG WILL NOT BITE!" He dragged his new owners out of the station and onto the top deck of a double-decker bus, where he sat and slobbered between us on the front seat all the way to Wrose.

He soon made friends with the neighbours children, but unfortunately he resented every dog he met, whatever shape or size, and fought them, resulting in inevitable veterinary bills from their owners. So he had to be kept on a lead out of doors. Indoors he soon got used to being left on his own for half a day while we went to work, and when I came back at lunchtime to exercise him, I would creep in and stand quietly in the hall – and a few moments later he would appear very sheepishly from the bedroom upstairs, before hurtling down to greet me.

When baby Michael arrived, Ferrari would walk proudly beside the pram, but one day while waiting outside a shop, his lead tied onto the pram, he spied another dog – and in a moment had shot after it, pulling the pram with him, and tipping the child out onto the pavement. Michael was unhurt though he cried lustily, and I had to soothe him, extricate the dogs and apologise to the other dog's owner, before going home as fast as possible. Ferrari was never allowed to guard the pram after that.

But he was allowed to run free on the Yorkshire moors, chasing the skylarks that soared high above his reach.

6. *Butch The Brindle Boxer 1968*

It is always hard when a much-loved dog passes away after a long and eventful life, and the house seemed so empty. Our two growing children, Mike and Clare, missed having a dog to greet them when they came home from school, and it was not long before they pleaded, “Can we look for a new dog, please?”

It was a small advertisement in the local Manchester Evening News that caught their attention. “Good home wanted for two-year old brindle boxer.”

Brian rang the number mentioned: “We would like to come and see your dog, please.”

The home in North Manchester was part of rather dingy terrace. We were invited inside to meet Butch. Unlike Ferrari who had been reddish brown all over, this one was a brindle, meaning he had stripes of different shades of brown. He was not slobbering, and seemed very friendly, keeping close to his young master, Paul, whose father explained that they had to part with Butch “for personal reasons.”

sliding; suddenly the ice gave way and he fell into the icy water. He struggled and struggled, but he could not get out.

Michael ran round the edge of the pool, calling to him and shouting for help. A man watching nearby said, "Look! There's a boat tied up over there – if we take that we can reach him." The little boat was quickly untied, and the rescuers smashed at the surrounding ice and managed to paddle towards the floundering dog. They reached him, grabbed his collar and hauled him back to the edge of the pool, where he clambered out, shook himself, and was smothered in hugs by a relieved and tearful Michael and Clare. People watching clapped their hands, and someone contacted the local newspaper...

The next day a photographer came to the house, and took pictures of Duke on the sofa between Michael and Clare. Michael was described as a hero, and Duke was the most recognised and pampered pooch in Poynton.

When a little stripy kitten was introduced into the family, and christened Tigger, Duke adopted her and allowed her to sleep beside him, snuggled up on his big soft bed. He really was a big softie!

8) Prince The Spaniel. 1982

My mother was unhappy and lonely in Cambridge, so she sold her house, we sold ours in Buckingham Road, and together we bought a big detached house with room for everyone, beside an old disused railway track that led down into the village (still Poynton!) or up into the open fields and old quarries. A marvellous place for a dog! But alas, Duke had gone to the big kennel in the sky. Tigger was now solely in charge of the family, and pottered up and down the Inclines, mostly with Granny Gilbert, or on her own, mouse-hunting.

Near Macclesfield in Cheshire is a farmhouse where dozens of abandoned cats and dogs are looked after until new owners come and take them home. It is called Windyways. One day an elderly spaniel called Prince was taken there because his owner had just died, and Prince was left on his own. It so happened that we had decided to visit Windyways, where a Summer Fair was being held, with stalls full of toys, books, gifts and old clothes, and an opportunity for visitors to look round the cattery and the kennels.

Clare saw Prince, and he looked at her. There was no doubt they spoke to each other. So Prince travelled home to the new house, and met Granny and Tigger. They all got on extremely well. Now all three went for walks together up and down the Inclines.

Prince was an old dog when he came into our lives, and he became very slow and arthritic. The family had a discussion, and agreed to find a suitable companion to cheer him up, and eventually to take over as No.1 Dog when Prince's long life should come to an end. Remembering how they had found Prince, the family decided to visit Windyways just once more.

9. Sophie The Terrier 1985

A little mongrel had recently given birth to five puppies at Windyways, all different colours and all demanding attention. We arrived with Clare and Michael to choose a new pet, to keep Prince, Tigger and Granny company.

Every kennel at the farm was occupied – big hounds, little terriers, furry and smooth-haired dogs. But these tiny little puppies were very beguiling. Clare pointed to a mostly white one with black patches – "That's the one, please!"

She had to wait several weeks while the puppies were weaned onto solid food, and at last we drove back to Windyways to fetch a now plump, bouncy little dog.

"What are we going to call her?" asked Michael. "Sophie" said Clare, "Sophie Maria."

It was not long before we realised that Sophie seemed to be scratching herself rather a lot. Looking closer, we found areas of her skin that were quite bald, and pink, even scaly. We took her to see the vet, who diagnosed a skin infection (obviously!) and prescribed a course of pills, some antiseptic baths and lots of daily ointment.

Fortunately neither Prince nor Tigger caught the infection, although they turned up their noses as the pungent puppy approached for a game.

Soon she stopped scratching, and the vet declared she was cured. At last the four friends with Michael and Clare could walk the Inclines again, and take a ball into the fields for Sophie to chase and, hopefully, to bring back.

Sophie went everywhere with us – to Dolgellau in Wales many times, up into the hills around Cheshire, and even to Poynton Show, where Sophie was entered for the Best Fancy Dress Dog, wearing a flowing white cape and with a gold crown on her head. She was not very comfortable pretending to be the Queen, but allowed herself to be paraded round the showground. She did not, alas, win a prize.

Sophie enjoyed a long and very happy life, and was perhaps the most important person in Michael and Clare's lives. She would be hard to replace.

10) Tessa The Collie Cross. 1999

It was like the end of an era – Granny, Tigger, and Sophie had all gone, Michael had settled in America with a young family, Clare was working as a nursery nurse and engaged to be married. So the first step Brian and I made was to move house (again!), still in Poynton, to Brookfield Avenue. The next move was to find someone to share it with us. Clare said “Windyways?” so off the three of us went. It was February 1999.

Once again there were so many dogs to choose from, so many sad faces that lit up when anyone passed near. In one run there were two collies, one all black, the other black and white. The kennel owner told us that someone walking in a public park in Stockport had seen a car pull in and park, let these two dogs out, watched them run off excitedly, and then the car just drove away.... It took several people two hours to catch both the dogs, put them into a van, and then take them up to Windyways.

Dogmatism

Who said, "The more I see of some people, the more I like my dog"? Not a kind thing to say – it gives the impression that dogs are usually inferior to humans, and anyone who is owned by a dog, on hearing this, would immediately muffle his canine's ears to prevent a justifiable retaliation with canine teeth. Dogs are very sensitive to criticism and many a rash human who mistakes a dog's silence for dumb stupidity would be unable to sit down comfortably for a week or more.

Dogs may not be able to talk, but they speak – with their eyes, their ears and their tails, in a language that can be understood the world over, and not just in canine circles.

Dogs are infinitely more honest than humans: a dog would never pretend delight at meeting someone he dislikes intensely, and then proceed to gossip about that person to the poodle next door. No, he instantly shows his animosity. Nor would he be coy in the presence of someone he likes. Far from it – he will fling his arms around his admirer in an ecstasy of joy and wash his (or her) face with passionate, very wet kisses.

Dogs are clever too. There was another ignorant human who said, "You cant teach an old dog new tricks." Well, you don't have to – he will soon teach himself when he realises that he can earn himself an extra muffin by standing on one leg, or hiding one of his old bones in Granny's nightie case.

Dogs learn all sorts of useful things – the days of the week for instance. On Mondays he will hide under the bed while the sheets are changed, and stay there with his paws over his ears so as not to hear the dreadful washing machine. On Tuesdays he sleeps on top of the bed, to avoid the fearsome vacuum cleaner. On Wednesdays he watches through the living room window for the dustbin men and shouts at them furiously until they go away. On Thursdays he entertains visitors for the Small Talk Coffee Morning, with a heart melting display of biscuit-begging and knee-leaning. On Fridays he helps to unpack the loaded weekend shopping bags, sampling a rasher of bacon here and a cheese portion there, and hiding the odd pork pie for a rainy day. On Saturdays and Sundays he follows Master around the house, and fetches his lead the moment Master looks like settling down with his wretched newspaper.

Dogs don't need clocks to tell the time – he knows exactly when the children are due home from school, the very moment his dinner should be served, the very moment his Master gets off the train every evening half a mile away.

He knows other things too – that a cake takes eight minutes to cool after leaving the oven, although the cook thinks it takes ten, and that those two minutes give him ample time to grab the cake and devour it at the bottom of the garden behind a rhododendron bush. He also knows the difference between "Come here, dog!" and "Come here, my pet!"

Dogs, like liquorice allsorts, come in different shapes, sizes and colours. Sometimes they come willingly, more often reluctantly, and they have to come at the end of a lead.

When they go, it is desperately sad. But hopefully they will have enjoyed a long, loving and greatly treasured life.

SHORT STORIES

To the Editor of the Saxon Chronicle, July 1034

Dear Sir,

It is with some trepidation that I write to advise you of a curious encounter that I had last week. I feel that the people of England should be made aware of this problem in case the perpetrator becomes completely unstable and causes civil war to begin.

Walking along the beach with my elkhound last Tuesday, I noticed a group of silken-clad gentlemen grouped around someone seated in a tall-backed armchair on the sands, by the water's edge. The tide was coming in, and the sea was actually lapping round the legs of the chair as well as the legs of the occupant. Then, to my horror, I noticed the crown perched on the occupant's head, and realised it was none other than our King, - Canute! He was gesticulating and shouting at the sea "Go back, go back!" But the tide continued to approach.

As the water reached his royal knees, the courtiers ran forward and lifted up the chair with the King still seated, and carried it up to the promenade. I distinctly heard the King say "There you are – you see what I mean? Not even the tide obeys my commands!"

I feel that this episode should be made public, but obviously I must ask you not to publish my name and address – the King shows no mercy to those who question his judgement. I would like to add that, as soon as the King departed, the tide did turn and began to withdraw, and I swear that the resultant hissing and clattering of the pebbles on the beach sounded very much like ironic laughter.

Yours truly,
Worried of Wessex

News Bulletin 1666

Good evening. Welcome to the PPC news at 6, in 1666.

His Majesty, King Charles, has issued his annual statement and is pleased to confirm that the dreadful plague that has devastated the people of London since last year seems to be on the wane. However, he still insists that pedestrians should continue to listen for the warning cry "Gardez Loo" and take evasive action to avoid contamination.

Our scientific reporter has informed us that a Cambridge professor has come up with an unlikely and rather ridiculous theory. Mr Newton describes it as the "law of gravitation", formulated when he observed an apple falling from a tree in the college garden!

I'm afraid we have breaking news – apparently a fire has broken out in Pudding Lane, and is spreading rapidly. It may have been caused by an apprentice baker, emulating the famous conflagration that occurred eight hundred years ago due to the carelessness of the unfortunate King Alfred.

I have been asked to advise all residents in the area to leave at once, and as this studio is only half a mile from Pudding Lane, we are closing down all broadcasting until further notice........alright, I'm coming..........

Four And Twenty Blackbirds.....

This song was first mentioned in a book entitled "Tommy Thumbs Nursery Rhymes", 1714. In that year, Queen Anne died and George 1st of Hanover became King. This is the story of the song, without mentioning any of the original characters or details.

Cook was delighted with her unusual recipe – it had only cost half a shilling and some cereal, and she was sure that her new master would appreciate her efforts. He was sorting his coin collection before lunch, while his wife was surreptitiously enjoying a vegetarian snack, when cook decided to test the pastry. She screamed with horror when the poultry within, far from being cooked, raised their heads and warbled their relief. One of them scrambled free and flew out of the window into the backyard. It surprised the girl pegging out the royal underwear by aiming for her scared face and taking a chunk out of her sniffer.......

From Our Correspondent In North Wales, 1811

This has been a really splendid day. After years of toil and determination, the great embankment has finally been completed, crossing the Traeth mawr for over a mile.

Thanks to the tireless work of many local men, tons of rock quarried from both sides has been transported in wagons pulled by teams of horses and tipped into the sea.

Finally, on September 17th, the gap has been closed. Today, Mr William Maddocks, MP, came to see for himself the completion of his dream. He was driven in his carriage to the site, but when the workmen saw him, they told the coachman to stop, then removed the horses, grabbed the shafts of the carriage, and dragged the coach with Mr Maddocks inside right across the embankment to the far end. Their pride was wondrous to behold, and their accomplishment will be seen and admired for years to come.

The Cob Opens 1811

My dearest sister, September 17th 1811

I do hope you are feeling better – it was so unfortunate that you should suffer another attack just as we were preparing to travel to Tremadoc to join the celebrations organised by Mr Maddocks.

I have some splendid news for you – this morning, Papa, Mama and I were invited to share Lord Reading's carriage, taking us in a procession with many others, to the special banquet being held half way along the new embankment, where we feasted on delicious slices of roast ox. My splendid news is that the handsome young man who travelled with us in the stagecoach from Holyhead was also in Lord Reading's carriage, and he introduced himself as Lord Reading's son, Alfred! Then at the ox roast, he asked me if I would honour him with a dance at the ball in Tremadoc this evening! But please tell no-one, especially not Grand-mama, or all Society will be informed. Curiously, last night we all witnessed a comet travelling through the night sky, and apparently it presages some great event – now, you and I know what it foretells!

Your loving sister,

Arabella

A Right Royal Ruction

Kate and William glared at the Queen, and said "But we want to call him Kevin!"

The Queen retorted "What a ridiculous idea! Every royal baby is always given special names that belonged to earlier royals – I would hope that you will reconsider, and name your baby Edward Richard Philip John Henry Charles."

Kate exclaimed "That's really impossible – I still think that Kevin is preferable. I mean, look at him! He's a gorgeous little Kevin! Would you like to hold for a moment, Ma'am?"

The Queen smiled. "Thank you, my dear. Yes, he is a dear little thing – looks just like his Daddy when he was a baby."

William was concerned. "No! Don't hold him upside down – he might be sick –oh, I warned you! All over your lovely pink suit!"

The Queen was appalled. "Er- that's ghastly – take him away please. I'll not bother to hold him again. I'll have to go and change my clothes. That should teach you to be more careful in future – and don't you dare call him Kevin, or, by George, I'll never speak to either of you again!"

William cried out "There, that's it! George!"

They all looked at each other, and smiled.

Bedtime Story

The sun dropped behind the hill, as a tear trickled down his cheek. He had always known that he would have to leave his mother one day, and find a new home in a distant place – a family tradition for many centuries. His little feet were sore from the rough road, and he was very thirsty, so he decided to find a quiet place beside a stream to rest.

Turning the corner he was confronted by a white cottage, with a sign swinging by the door- "Travellers Rest". He knew he was not old enough to ask for a drink in a public house, but surely there might be some half-full glasses on the tables in the garden. He stooped low, and crept through the gate without being seen. He was right! Several pint pots glinted in the half-light, and he reached up and lifted down the first one. Whatever it was, it tasted delicious, so he tried the second one, then the third...Smiling happily, he decided to stay in the garden for the night, and continue his journey early in the morning. Just one belch before he settled down – he opened his mouth and released a huge puff of smoke and flames.

A customer inside the pub was looking through the window and exclaimed "I don't believe it! There's a dragon in the garden – and breathing fire!"

"Nonsense – you're drunk!" scoffed his friends.

"Never mind" said the landlady, "That is a Designated Smoking Zone."

The little dragon curled up on the bench and drifted off to sleep.

A Friend for George

The bus was late again. George felt really miserable, knowing that Miss Bossyboots would make him stand in front of the class yet again as a punishment, even though he couldn't help being late for school. The girls would snigger.... Living half way up a mountain, miles from the village didn't help. At least he had done his homework this time, the story of George and the Dragon.

He was suddenly aware of someone standing behind him, who was muttering to himself, something about being hungry. The stranger spoke: "And I could eat you up right now little boy!"

George turned, and stared at him. "Oh no you don't!" he said very bravely, trying to look older than ten and braver than he felt. The stranger laughed. "You're afraid of me really, just like everyone else. Nobody likes me – I don't know why-" then he began to cry. "I don't have any friends!"

George felt sorry for him. "Perhaps it's because you look so fierce, and when you open your mouth and breathe fire all over them, they just run away."

The stranger looked at George. "You're not running away! Aren't you afraid of me?"

"No – not really. I'm sure you are quite a nice dragon – don't you like people?"

"Don't really know any people – my grandfather had a bad experience with people. This maiden was tied to a tree, ready for his lunch, and then a human appeared on horseback and killed Granddad with a sword. So ever since we avoid people, and if they come too near, we breathe fire all over them!"

"Perhaps if you talked to them, like you're talking to me, and even smiled at them, you might make friends."

“Do you have friends?”

“Not many. Perhaps we could be friends together?”

“Why, yes! I’d like that!” the dragon replied, and he smiled happily.

Just then the bus drew up. George turned to say goodbye to his new friend, but he had gone…

“Hurry up, George” said the bus driver, “Talking to yourself again? Jump on – we’ll make up time going down hill. You won’t be late.”

Flight to Freedom

Just after midnight, she woke to hear the owl calling from the woods behind the cottage. Then she remembered – the fearful, dangerous adventure that she had planned for this day. She was going to run away! No-one had remembered her tenth birthday, they had fussed over the new arrival instead, and because she had hit him, she had been sent to bed without any supper.

Her foster parents were snoring in the next room as usual – they would not notice her absence for several hours, perhaps they never would...She got dressed in the dark, put her mobile phone in her coat pocket, and crept downstairs. She would need some money – the little safe where her foster mother kept the milk money was on a shelf in the pantry beside the egg timer. She tried to open it, but did not know how. Depressed but still determined, she unlocked the front door, closing it silently behind her, and walked out into the lane.

The darkness wrapped round her as she began the long walk to freedom, her heart beating like a metronome. Something was standing in her way, an invisible creature that bleated as she approached. Only a lost black sheep, looking for friends like herself.

As she approached the top of the hill, a sudden flash of light blinded her – terrified she stood in the middle of the road, reliving her favourite story on television, suddenly convinced that the Tardis was about to land, and Dr Who was coming to take her away. The light grew brighter and hurtled straight towards her – panicking, she ran to the side of the road, as the car raced just a few feet away.

The driver caught a glimpse of a small girl in his headlights, braked sharply and managed to stop. He got out and ran back towards the child, who was crying inconsolably on the verge.

“What are you doing out here at this time of night?” he shouted.

She could not speak. “Where do you live? Let me take you home.” She pointed down the road towards the cottage, and allowed him to lift her into the car. They stopped outside and she ran up the path, without thanking the man, who drove away, puzzled and perturbed.

She tiptoed upstairs and went back to bed. She never told her foster parents, and they never found out, about her flight to freedom.

On Reflection

Each day reflects the image of the one before, week by week into the distance. Daily routines, hour by hour, unchanging like the tide that regularly ebbs and flows outside my window. But then a precious moment comes and makes the tedium seem worthwhile. Silently, six brown cygnets arrive in dutiful procession behind their proud parents and cruise below the harbour wall to please the summer visitors. Then today I picked the first plump blackberry while my dog plunged into the tangled undergrowth. I listen to my evening blackbird whistling again and again "half a pound of tuppeny rice...." I take a walk through the village on some excuse, and chance to meet a friend with news of others, and we laugh together. Best of all, every day the swallows entertain – dancing, swirling, circling, swooping down to the surface of the still water to see their own image, then up and away, and round again.

Yet when the wind whips the chocolate waves, still they come and swoop in search of supper. The tedium will return of course, but small glimpses of stolen moments will filter into my mind and make me smile with secret joy.

He's Coming to the WI!

Mrs. Ogilvie could hardly wait to get to the WI meeting.

"He's coming!" she shouted excitedly as she rushed into the side room of the Ganolfan.

"Who's coming?" demanded Mrs Frost.

"Why, HIM of course!"

"Don't be ridiculous!" said Mrs Frost "– He's much too busy."

Mrs Jones muttered "I thought he was still in prison."

Mrs Ogilvie frowned. "Not him, dear – HIM!"

The Secretary, Mrs Blott thumped the table. "Come along ladies, do sit down. We should have started the meeting ten minutes ago. But before I read the minutes of the last meeting, could we clear up exactly **who** is coming?"

Mrs. Ogilvie was getting annoyed. "Surely you remember that Mrs Adkins told us that her famous nephew was hoping to come and visit her?"

Mrs Owen was puzzled. "But she died – last week!"

Mrs Ogilvie continued – "Exactly – so her nephew is bound to be coming to her funeral, and as we will all be going to the church and to the crematorium afterwards, we shall be able to see him, and maybe speak to him. Won't that be wonderful?"

Mrs. Perkins sighed "Oh yes. I've read all his books."

"Don't be silly" said Mrs Ogilvie, "He's not a writer. He's a member of that pop group, the Wrong Direction. He's the hairy one in the middle – Robbie something."

Mrs Stott muttered "What rubbish" She stood up and turned her back on Mrs.Ogilvie. Then she looked up at the ceiling and announced in her usual superior tone: "Mrs Adkins told me that her nephew was a Rabbi living in Poland."

There was silence in the room. The secretary spoke firmly "I think we can establish finally that the nephew is not Robbie from the Wrong Direction but a Rabbi from the other direction. I personally think that it is most unlikely that he will be coming to his aunt's funeral anyway. Can we get on with the meeting, please?"

Mrs. Ogilvie was distraught and embarrassed. She had been so certain....at last she would actually meet a real pop star. She hurried out of the room and began to sort the cups and saucers in the kitchen, and in her haste tipped over a plate of home made cakes, which crashed onto the floor, and lay in a tangled mess of china and chocolate muffins at her feet.

"Damn!" she cried, "What an idiot I am!"

The Window

All day the rain and wind battered against my tall window, so intensely that my treasured view disappeared for hours on end. Eventually the rain subsided slightly and I could just see the anchored boats swerving, dipping, and swirling, as the gale tried maliciously to overturn them. But the ropes held fast onto the buoys, as the tall masts swayed dangerously high above. The giant waves continued to batter the stone walls, leaping up against the arches of the old bridge. Then back came the rain, obscuring everything once more.

I made myself a pot of tea, then sat and filled in the daily crossword, trying to ignore the commotion of the elements outside.

Suddenly I realised that everything was quiet and looked out of my window. The boats were still, unmoving, their masts pointing triumphantly to the dark sky. The waves were now merely ripples; the tide had turned, and slowly crept back out to sea.

Raindrops still splashed onto my battered plant pots, one of which had succumbed to the wind and was lying on its side. Two pigeons emerged from their hiding place across the river, and began pecking behind the pots, where I daily scatter crumbs for them, also for my pied wagtail, my robin and my sparrow. No seagull is allowed anywhere near.

As the day drew silently to a close, the harbour lights gained strength and cast their reflections into the sea. I drew the curtains, glad that the storm was over.

My Early Life

I was born one May morning in the warm family nest among the reeds of a pond. My mother came and sat on me for several days until I was able to break open my shell and peer out at the strange world surrounding me. My older brothers and sisters encouraged me to climb out onto the bank, where I waddled after them as they plunged into the big lake. I did manage to swim, but try as I might, I found I could not quack like everyone else. It was a great disappointment to the family. They were also concerned that my feathers were brown rather than yellow, and that my neck was longer than anyone else's. They began to tease me, and call me unkind names, so after a few weeks of misery, I decided to run away. I managed to find plenty of weed to eat, and made a comfortable bed for myself at the edge of the lake, where I spent most of each day practising my swimming. My feathers slowly turned from brown to white, and my neck grew longer and longer. My reflection in the lake told me that I was ugly, and I felt very ashamed of myself.

Then one day a flock of big white birds flew down and landed feet first on the lake quite near. They stared at me, and then one came over and honked. Guess what I did? Yes, I honked back! I could speak at last! I suddenly realised that I looked just like this new friend; in fact we could have been brothers. Perhaps I never was a duck at all, even though I had been brought up mistakenly by a kind foster mother.

Joyfully, I stretched my big white wings, curved my graceful neck, and glided out to join my real welcoming family.

Billy

In his eyes, she saw only darkness. She stared at him, unable to understand why he had changed so unexpectedly, so suddenly. The glimmer of love had gone, replaced by this look that she could only interpret as guilt. What had he done? Had he betrayed her trust? Or had she unwittingly given him cause to make him feel that he was no longer her one and only love?

She began to cry, and put her hands out to touch him. He flinched, turned and left the room. Desperately, she followed him – he went into the kitchen and stood still, looking at her. Now she was certain – he was guilty, but of what? She trusted him so completely, certain he would always love her as deeply as she loved him.

"Tell me, darling, please – what is troubling you?"

Only then did he turn his head towards the corner of the room. There, motionless, in a tangle of feathers, lay the remains of a young sparrow.

"Oh Billy!" she cried, "What have you done?"

Billy moved towards her, and pressed himself close. His eyes were filled with shame, as he looked up at her, imploring forgiveness.

Natural instinct had overcome him, and he had pounced on the little bird, expecting it to fly out of his reach. But instead he had trapped it in his paws, and then, panicking, had carried it indoors, trusting that his beloved mistress would be able to restore it to life. But alas, it was dead.

She knew he must have killed it by mistake, and recognised his desperate appeal for help. She smiled, picked him up, and cuddled him tenderly, murmuring "It's alright, darling – Mummy understands. We will take the little birdie into the garden, and bury him under the rose bush."

Billy looked deep into her eyes, pressed his head against her cheek, and began to purr. Love and trust encircled them both once more.

The Secret of Ballast Island – A True Story 1

Once upon a time, about seventy years ago, Little Dorothy picked her way across to Ballast Island, a lonely place not far away from the family's cottage near the Cob, and only accessible at low tide. She often went there, and would sit on the stones, picturing in her mind the big ships from foreign lands offloading their unwanted ballast just there before entering Porthmadog dock to load up with slate to take back home. At one time there had been a house on the island, and the man who lived there ran a small railway with a wagon in which he transferred quantities of ballast from the far end of the island and deposited it nearer the mainland. During the Second World War, troops billeted in the area would use the house for target practice, shooting at it from the Cob.

Little Dorothy put her hand down beside her big stone seat, and felt something round and smooth. She gripped it and pulled it up. It was black and shiny, with what looked like round hooks protruding from it. She scraped at it with her fingers, but could not dislodge the thick tar covering the rock – if that is what it was. So she left it there and went home, and forgot all about it.

Years later, young Dorothy scrambled onto the rocks below the Cob, and sat watching the seabirds circling in the wind. Her hand fell against something hard, and she realised it was another lump of black stuff with similar hook-like protuberances. Once again she could not scrape off the tar, so she threw it into a large, empty, rusty water tank that had been abandoned below on the edge of the Cob. The object landed with a clunk and a splash.

Quite recently, Dorothy and her husband returned to retire in Porthmadog. Their daughter often walks her dogs on Ballast Island. It is very overgrown today with trees and shrubs, some from the far countries that created the island with their unwanted ballast, and many visitors and local residents visit it for its unusual variety of flora and fauna.

Watching the Antiques Roadshow one Sunday, Dorothy was astonished when one of the visitors placed a familiar lump of black stone on the table for the expert to explain and value. At first he was unable to do so, but sent the object to a laboratory, and at last the mystery was explained.

Several hundred years ago, battling forces fired cannonballs at enemy gallcons, setting fire to the caulked woodwork, melting the tar which fell into the hold beneath, covering everything within, including the treasure chests full of money. The detritus then floated away with the tide.

Scientists managed to remove the black covering, to reveal the gold coins that had been trapped for generations.

Dorothy knows that the old rusty tank disappeared years ago, and wonders whether any more black objects still lie undiscovered on Ballast Island. Maybe explorers with metal detectors have found and removed them, but Dorothy feels sure that Ballast Island still keeps its secrets well hidden.

The Knock at the Door

Someone was knocking at the door. Her heart missed a beat. She shivered, suddenly afraid. Only last week, the old man next door had been burgled: he had opened the door to two strange men who tied him up and then ransacked his cottage for anything they thought they could sell – his war medals, his silver framed photographs, his gold watch and chain. They also took away his will to live.

There – another knock. She clutched at the arms of her chair to stop her body shaking. Then she noticed that Benjy, her old collie, was sitting bolt upright in his basket by the fireplace, staring at the door – but he wasn't barking. He always barked if someone knocked at the door, but not this time.

"What is it, Benjy?" she whispered, "Who is it?"

Benjy wagged his tail, still staring at the door. A terrible thought struck her: the only person that Benjy never barked at had been John, her son. They had been to place flowers on his grave only that morning. Was it him, poor dead John, standing outside, waiting to return?

She began to cry, but forced herself to rise out of her chair and walk, very slowly and fearfully, to the door. She took a deep breath and opened it.

Standing on the doorstep was a young lad – not John, but Billy, the grandson of old Mr Brown from next door. He smiled up at her.

"Hallo!" he said, "I wondered if you would let me take Benjy for a walk again?"

Before she could compose herself to reply, Benjy rushed across and was wagging his tail in anticipation.

"Of course you can, dear – any time. But don't bother to knock in future – just walk in."

PLAYLETS

A Small Diamond –

A "radio" play for five voices: It takes place in 1730, in a horse-drawn carriage (the Mail coach) in Yorkshire.

CAST: Nellie, a maid. Lady Green, her employer. Mrs. Matilda Palmer. The Coachman. Dick Turpin.

Nellie: Is this seat taken? Oh, I do apologise, Lady Green – I failed to recognise you, it is so dark in this carriage after the sunlight outside.

Lady G: Pray do sit beside me, Nellie – this is your first visit to York, is it not? I trust your father will meet you at the coaching inn?

Nellie: Oh yes, Lady Green – I believe York is no place for a young girl to visit unaccompanied.

Lady G: Quite so. I never go anywhere without my footman. He is seated on the roof with our luggage. I understand that another lady is hoping to share the mail coach with us today. Ah – here she comes. My, what a pretty hat! Rather too pretty for such an elderly person.

M.P: I hope I have not kept you all waiting. Would you mind holding my basket, dear, while I climb aboard? Thank you so much. There, all in! You can go now, coachman!

Lady G: Let me introduce myself – I am Lady Green of Bank Manor, and this young lady is one of my parlour maids. She is visiting her family in York. And you are?

M.P. Oh, my name is...um, it is hard to concentrate with the bumping and shaking of the carriage, and the thudding of the horse's hooves. Ah, yes – my name is Mrs Matilda Palmer, and I am returning home after a pleasant holiday with my grandchildren. And in this basket – thank you, my dear, I'll take it from you now. In this basket is my precious little companion.

Nellie: He's very sweet – he is a Jack Russell, isn't he?

M.P. Very good, dear. Yes, he is only a pup still, but he is fiercely devoted to me. Careful if you stroke him – let him sniff your hand first.

Lady G: Mrs. Palmer, I must protest – even our King does not allow animals to ride with him in his royal carriage. Besides, I have a dislike of small vicious animals.

Nellie: I feel sure he will behave himself perfectly during the journey.

Lady G: Humph! Oh – what is happening? The horses are rearing up- the coach man has lost control!

M P : Oh my good lord – preserve me!

Nellie: Hold tight, ladies – perhaps a fox ran across the road. But we are stopping – there's a man trying to open the door ....help!

D.T.; Well well, ladies, may I present myself; Dick Turpin, here to relieve you of your most precious possessions.

Lady G.; Don't point that gun at me, Sir – Coachman! Come here at once!

D.T.: He can't come, I'm afraid, Madam. He and your footman have run off across the fields like a couple of hares. You, Madam, what do you have hidden in that basket?

M.P,: Don't you DARE come near my precious Diamond....

D.T.: Diamond, eh? Hand it over! AAAh! Get it off me...

M.P: Good boy – hang on, my darling!

Nellie: That will teach you, you horrible man – just let me PUSH you out of the door – he's gone!

Lady G. Well done, dear – and well done, little Diamond. Ah, the coachman is back – what happened to the highwayman?

Coach: He is in the ditch, Ma'am – nursing his damaged hand. We will be resuming our journey shortly. May I say, your ladyship, your bravery and resilience has completely amazed me. To what do we owe your deliverance?

Lady G. Well, sir, it was entirely due to a small.....Diamond.

Over The Garden Wall

A man is carefully weeding the flower bed at the base of the dividing wall. A woman peers over the garden wall.

SHE Oh, hello! You must be the new owner of no 13!

HE (**looking up at her**) Ah- yes! Just moved in. I take it you are my next door neighbour. My name is Dick.

SHE Oh fancy that! I thought it might be – after all I just spotted you! (**she laughs** a**wkwardly**) Spotted dick? Ah well.... I am Fanny.

HE Otherwise known as Funny? Sorry – I didn't mean to be offensive.

SHE Oh that's alright – no offence taken. I do tend to see the funny side of everything. Used to annoy my Freddie no end.

HE Freddy?

SHE My late husband – he passed away several years ago, thank goodness. We didn't get on.

HE I'm sorry to hear that. I've never had a wife so perhaps I'm lucky.

SHE No lady friend?

HE No – just my dog, Tipsy. She's the only companion I need.

SHE That's nice. Where is she? In kennels?

HE No – she's over there – by the apple tree. Digging like mad, I'm afraid.

SHE (**alarmed**) Digging? Oh my God! Do stop her at once!

HE Oh? Sorry – but it is my garden, and I don't mind where she digs.

SHE Anywhere but there – for goodness sake, pull her away!

HE I wonder why you are so worried? What do you think she might find? Tipsy!

Come here. What have you got in your mouth? It looks like…like –hells bells!

SHE (**petrified**) What is it? What has she got?

HE I do believe it's….. a daffodil bulb.

SHE Oh thank God! I was so afraid……

HE Yes, you were, weren't you? Don't tell me – let me guess. I can see it all – one dark night you threw your husband's body over the garden wall, then a spade, and climbed over yourself. You dug a big hole under the apple tree, put him in it then covered it up with soil from this flower bed. Am I right?

SHE That's incredible! That's exactly what happened. You just left out the bit where I poisoned him at supper time, waited for him to die, then when it was quite dark did just what you described. The occupants were away next door, so I knew no-one would see me. So how on earth could you have known?

HE Simple. The house WAS empty – except for the burglar upstairs. That was me. Very profitable it was too. And watching your little exploit was most entertaining.

SHE You're a burglar! A criminal…..

HE So are you! If you don't tell, I won't either. This could be the beginning of a very pleasant and close relationship, Fanny.

SHE Yes, it could….Would you like to pop over and join me in a cup of tea?

HE Well, in the circumstances, I'd much rather you came over here and let me make the tea!

SHE Oh. very well – give me your hand, Dicky bird!

Mayhem in Pantoland

3 old ladies, 1 man and 1 wolf

The curtain rises, to reveal a rustic country scene, with two seats at either side of the stage, a backdrop painted with a distant castle, cardboard cut-outs of bushes in the foreground, and the large figure of a WOLF sleeping on a bench centre stage. The PRINCE enters, looking around with a troubled expression on his handsome face, and sees the WOLF.

PRINCE:- Wake up, you! **(Wolf growls)** Have you seen a pretty girl dressed in rags wandering around here ? Only I have got one of her shoes.

WOLF (**growling again**) She tasted very nice – like strawberry trifle – only she wasn't in rags: she had a pretty white dress and lovely golden hair. She said she thought I was a bear! So I gobbled her up. Now, go away and let me sleep.

PRINCE Disgraceful behaviour! I don't allow wild animals in my kingdom – except of course my pet clockodile. What is this place, anyway? I seem to have lost my way since my equine sat-nav threw me down the road. Some strange looking individuals living around here - they all ignored me. I'm not used to being ignored. A fat farmer who looked like a huge egg sitting on a wall, and seven little men with pickaxes looking for Snow – I ask you! In mid summer! And then a girl with extremely long hair climbing a beanstalk!

WOLF This is Pantoland – we had a bit of an earthquake yesterday and everything is topsy-turvy. Just go away and leave me in peace. Look – that old woman just arriving – she might know something- ask her!

(Old woman enters with a basket of apples)

PRINCE Excuse me, old crone, give me one of your apples. I've not eaten since Christmas and feel somewhat peckish.

OLD W. You can't have one – they are for a Certain Person, when I find her – she's wandered off somewhere with a woodcutter. And don't call me Old Crone – under this disguise I am a royal personage.

PRINCE. Oh yes? Well under this disguise I am really a chimney sweep!

(Two ladies have entered and overheard this last remark. They are very ugly and in drag)

UGLY SISTER 1 Really? We've just the job for you! Our wretched serving girl has driven off in a pumpkin, of all things, and left the kitchen in a terrible mess – cinders everywhere – we'll show you the way to our castle!

PRINCE You are mistaken – I only said that I was a chimney sweep as a joke! In fact I am Prince Charming from the other side of the rainbow.

UGLY SISTERS (**ecstatic**) Prince? Oh, how marvellous! We have been waiting for you! Come along with us, ducky!

They grab the Prince and he tries to fend them off, then the wolf wakes up and charges at them and the sisters run off in different directions. The Prince dusts himself down and says)

PRINCE Thank you, Mr Wolf. You have saved my life. How can I ever repay you?

WOLF Easy – just give me a kiss and see what happens....

PRINCE Will you turn into a beautiful princess?

WOLF Perhaps – or more likely a sheep. Your name is really Bo Peep, isn't it my precious?

(The Prince screams and rushes away pursued by the laughing wolf.)

The End!

The Swiss Holiday

Ethel and Ivy are old friends, and often go on holiday together.

They are on Eurostar as it approaches St. Pancras station.

ETHEL: Thank goodness that's over – what a journey! I couldn't see anything out of the window, the train was going so fast. And that long tunnel! I kept thinking about all that sea just above our heads…suppose there was a crack somewhere and it all poured in…!

IVY: I know, I didn't like it either. My coffee wasn't very nice – so bitter. Should have asked for tea. And all those people jabbering in a foreign language in the buffet car – so rude.

ETHEL: Yes, it was the same in the hotel – I kept bumping into that big fat man smelling of tobacco every time I went up in the lift: couldn't understand a word he said either.

IVY: Mind you, our room wasn't too awful, though we didn't have a view of the mountains, just the pub next door – what a noise they made every night! Didn't we ask for a room with a view when we booked?

ETHEL: Of course we did, and that was the view we got! I shall complain to the travel company.

IVY: They were wrong about the excursions too – we had to walk miles from the coach park to get to any shops, and all they sold were frilly embroidered blouses – most unsuitable for ladies of a certain age.

ETHEL: I think the worst day was that trip up the mountain in that funny..funny carriage thing – funicular or something.

IVY: You mean gondola?

ETHEL ; No, silly, those are like punts, in Venice. Anyway, we got in last, so we had to sit facing straight down the mountain – and as the church steeple and houses shrank and disappeared below us, I felt really sick and scared.

IVY: I thought I was going to be sick too, but that was the cheese tart we'd had for breakfast. Disgusting.

ETHEL: Then when we got to the top, we had to sit in the station shelter for ages because of the driving snow – ooh, it was cold! So we came back down as soon as we could, but it was hours before the coach came back to pick us up.

IVY; We're arriving at St Pancras – better start getting ready to get out.

(They stand up and make their way to the end section of the carriage where all the luggage is stored. They finally locate their own suitcases – Ethel dislodges hers and inadvertently drops it onto a fellow passenger's foot. Ivy drags hers towards the door, tripping over someone's walking stick. At last the train stops, and eventually they clamber down onto the platform, commandeer a trolley, and set off towards the exit, where a familiar figure is waiting for them, waving excitedly as she sees them approach.)

ETHEL: Why, isn't that our Rosie? Thank goodness – I hope she's brought the car so we wont have to find a taxi.

(She hurries to Rosie, and they embrace)

ROSIE: Welcome home, Aunties! So what was it like? Did you have a wonderful holiday in Switzerland?

ETHEL (beaming) Oh, yes – it was really lovely! We thoroughly enjoyed every minute of it, didn't we, Ivy?

IVY:- Yes indeed – can't wait to go back again one day! Such lovely people, lovely views, lovely hotel. Even better than Blackpool.

"Where Shall We Go Next?"

Darby and Joan are sitting in their front room, surrounded by holiday brochures.

JOAN – It will be nice to have a real change this year. Oh! I like this one!

DARBY – What's that then?

JOAN - Luxury cruise to the Caribbean. The ship's got two dining rooms, a swimming pool, bingo every night and Old Tyme Dancing!

DARBY – Very nice. We get all that at Scarborough.

JOAN - Don't be silly, dear. Think about it – a big ship going thousands of miles across the sea...

DARBY – You don't like the sea. Whenever we've been in a boat, you've been sick.

JOAN - Well, it would be different in a big ship – less bumpy.

DARBY - Anyhow, we don't do swimming, or dancing. And I hate bingo. Now, this one looks much more promising.

JOAN - What's that then?

DARBY - Coach trip to Italy. Visiting Rome, Pisa, Venice – and lots of little mountain villages in between with cobbled streets and donkeys.

JOAN - You'd never manage cobbled streets with your legs. And you know what big cities are like – full of foreigners and not a decent public loo anywhere.

DARBY - Still, make a nice change from Scarborough.

JOAN - And another thing – you can't get fish and chips in Italy.

DARBY - 'Course you can!

JOAN – No you can't – Fred told me. All pasta and snails.

DARBY – That's France.

JOAN - Same thing – rubbish food.

DARBY – How about Scotland?

JOAN – Don't like bagpipes.

DARBY - Wales?

JOAN - Don't like mountains.

DARBY – There's no pleasing you, is there?

JOAN - Well, if we don't go on a cruise, or a coach trip anywhere, where else can we go for our holiday this year?

(They turn away from each other, frowning. After a few minutes, they look up and glance across at their partner. They speak together;-)_

DARBY AND JOAN - Scarborough?

Cinderella (In Verse)

CAST: - Cinderella, Fairy Godmother, Two Ugly Sisters, and Prince

Scene One: - Cinderella is sitting by the fire, crying:

CINDERS:- Oh, what a miserable girl I am!
My ugly sisters, Mabel and Pam,
Have gone to the Palace to meet the Prince –
They-re having a Ball – it makes me wince.
Perhaps if I wish, loud and clear,
My Fairy Godmother will appear.

FAIRY G.:- Ah Cinders! I was passing by
When I heard your plaintive little cry.
I'll wave my wand – the rags you wore
Are now a gown by Christian Dior!

CINDERS :- Oh, thankyou – to the Ball I'll go –
But it's a longish walk, you know.

FAIRY G:- No fear – your hamster in its cage
Will become a horse and carri-age!

(She turns to the audience and speaks to them quite seriously: -

"You will need to realise the complexities involved in actually performing this dramatic transformation- no doubt when we transfer to the West End, we shall have magnificent costumes, scenery, lighting, full orchestra, majestic staircase, and with luck a real Prince...however, for now – on with the show!"

SCENE TWO – The palace, the Prince is dancing with Mabel and Pam

PRINCE:- This is turning out to be
A disappointing Ball for me –
I'd hoped to find a beautiful wife,
But I've never seen anything uglier all my life!
These women will not leave me alone –
I wish I'd brought my mobile phone!
I could have rung for the fire brigade
Who would have hurried to my aid.
But lo! What a gorgeous sight I see!
Beautiful girl, will you dance with me?

CINDERS :- With pleasure, good sir! How my heart is beating...
Alas, the time is quickly fleeting -
When midnight strikes, my frock will fall....
Then I must hurriedly leave the Ball.
But hark! The clock is striking twelve!
Dear Prince, I really have to leave!
But I cannot run in these ghastly shoes –
I'll kick them off.....please excuse!

PRINCE:- Dear girl, I do not know your name
But I shall find you just the same.
I'll take these shoes and try them on
Every girl in my kingdom.

SCENE THREE:- Ugly sisters trying vainly to put on the shoes which the Prince is forcing onto their feet.

MABEL:- Push harder, Sir, I know they'll fit.
I'll scrunch my toes up just a bit...
OW! The pain I have to suffer
To convince the Prince to be my lover!

PAM:-My turn now – this one's just right..
Well, just a teensy weensy bit tight....
My heel is sticking out behind!
A better fit you'll never find!

CINDERS:- Excuse me, Sir, please let me try.
My ugly sisters can but sigh,
They have such large and smelly feet,
But mine are dainty, soft and sweet.....

PRINCE:- Pray, try, young lady. Ah, behold
How well these shoes your feet enfold!
(That is a really awful line!)
But never mind – will you be mine?

CINDERS:- Of course, dear Prince, let us be wed –
Or we could just stay here instead?
That would save that final scene
With guests, a vicar, King and Queen,
Those flashy costumes, curtain calls,
A backdrop of Niagara Falls –
Let's just end this here and now –
So all together – take a bow!

POEMS

Crabbing

Up comes the line with its captured crab,
As the children scream and retreat –
So Dad has to loosen its claws with a stick
And drop the crab into a bucket.
So why do the children keep trying all day,
Leaning over to dangle the bait,
While Dad fills the bucket with every new catch
A job that the children just hate?
At last the full bucket is tipped over the edge
And the terrified crabs are returned,
Only to find that they're caught yet again,
Several times, every day, and then spurned.
Perhaps they are screaming and shouting for help –
Nobody listens or cares....
So long as the children are happy themselves
Then crabbing will go on for years.

Peace

In the midst of darkness there
May come a moment of peace,
When the clouds reveal a tranquil sky
And suddenly a shaft of sunlight
Brings a rainbow into your day
Warming, just like a friendly smile.

The Vending Machine

The boy waddled up to the vending machine –
A more gorgeous selection he never had seen!
Chocolates, and crisps, coco cola and juice,
His mouth was watering – which one to choose?
At last he decided, put a coin in the slot.
As his fat finger hovered, a voice shouted "What?
You cannot be serious, little plump lad,
Everything here is fattening and bad!"
The boy was appalled, but he shouted "You're mean!
You're just an ignorant Offending Machine!"

At the Back of the Drawer

At the back of the drawer in somebody's home,
Lies something beneath an old sock,
With hankies and undies, a brush and a comb,
Shoved in when she heard a sharp knock.
Only the postman – a parcel to sign.
Then later a trip to the shop,
She meets a few friends, and the weather is fine –
A phone-call, some gossip to swap.
Forgotten completely, the thing in the drawer,
It may stay there for several years.
One day she will find it when ageing and poor,
Too late to shed any tears.
For this is the lottery ticket unclaimed,
Worth millions or so it is said,
It could have been hers – she should not be blamed,
For charities got it instead.

Mike Roberts, The Iron Man

Clad in iron from head to toe,
Mike Roberts made a fiercesome foe,
Sneering with hate in the wrestling ring
And throwing opponents out with a fling.
Of course, wearing armour was rather unfair,
As all other wrestlers were virtually bare.
But it happened that during an infamous bout
Big Giant Haystacks threw Mike Roberts out!
His armour was dented to such a degree
They used a tin opener to set the man free.
The audience roared with cruel delight
At this highly amusing but shameful sight.
Mike got up slowly and crawled away,
And has never been heard of since that day.

Christmas Comes But Once a Year

Thank goodness, I must say!
With gifts to buy and cards to send
It's not for just a day.
From August when the shops go mad
And dress their staff as gnomes,
And garish glitter fills the stores
To decorate our homes.
Then in December we are filled
With food that makes us fat,
At lunches, dinners, teas and Do's
And drinks that knock us flat.
We like to share it with our friends
And families from afar,
Or call round to the Nursing Home
To hug dear Grand-papa.
How many of us will that day
Remember, if we're able,
The little baby laid to sleep
With his mother in a stable......

Cold Hands

She waited, certain he would come-
Her heart was beating fast,
Misunderstandings overcome,
He'd hold her tight at last.
Then in he walked, but frowned and said
"It's over!" Out he swept –
She rose and screamed "I wish you dead!
You're so cold, Hans!" she wept......

A Special Encounter

Leo and his Mum were strolling in the park
When he thought he heard a familiar bark –
He quickly turned round, expecting to see
His long lost friend – but it wasn't to be.
Biting his lip, he followed his Mum
Who wondered why he was looking so glum.
"I thought I heard....very silly, I know.
She'll never come back, but I miss her so!"
His Mum put her arms around her lad.
"I know, my darling, we all feel sad –
But I think I know a really good way
To make you happy, this very day.
There's somebody here I want you to meet –
In fact, it's an early Birthday treat."
Just then a lady came into view
And waved to Mum who waved back too.
Trotting beside her, to Leo's surprise,
Was a dear little spaniel with big brown eyes.
"You must be Leo," said the lady with a smile,
"I've known your mother for quite a while.
She told me that you had lost your friend,
So we wondered if we could recommend
A solution for Leo and also for Boo
For he is homeless and lonely too."
But Leo was hugging his new furry pal
Who was wagging his tail and grinning as well.
Leo's Mum thanked the lady, who gave her the lead.
It had been a rewarding arrangement indeed.
So the boy and his dog were both happy at last
And their previous loneliness all in the past.

The Train Pulled out of the Station…

The train pulled out of the station
And chugged its way down to the sea.
The smoke from its funnel rose upward
And shrouded each woodland tree.
The fireman threw coal on the fire
While the driver was watching ahead,
And Linda began to go faster
As down to Porthmadog she sped.
She rounded a curve between fields,
And everything seemed to be fine,
When all of a sudden the driver exclaimed
"There's a silly old sheep on the line"!
He dragged on the brakes, and, as the train slowed,
It shuddered again and again,
While the panicking sheep ran as fast as it could
Just inches away from the train.
The banks were quite high either side of the line
So it had to keep going along,
But at last it managed to squeeze through a hedge,
Watched by an anxious throng.
The driver relaxed and gave Linda more power
So she soon gathered speed on her way,
While the sheep stood aside and watched her depart,
And never forgot that bad day.

Trouble at the Zoo

The gorilla knocked on the wardrobe door –
His knuckles were getting really sore.
The zoo man inside shouted “Go away!
I really don’t want to come out and play.
Besides, it’s nearly feeding time,
Lovely fruit salad with bananas and lime.”
The gorilla muttered and sat on the floor,
He didn’t want fruit for lunch any more,
But he fancied a piece of the zoo-keeper’s arm…
So he patiently waited, quite happy and calm.

Cat Encounter

The cat sat on the mat and she was purring with delight,
Remembering the handsome Tom that she had met last night.
He was visiting her garden – she had seen him in the dark
So went to reprimand him, but ah! there was a “spark”!
They looked into each other’s eyes, and suddenly they knew
That loneliness was over, and love between them grew.
But somebody was calling “Tom! It’s time for bed!”
He had to go, but turned to her and quietly he said
“Meet me tomorrow?” “Yes, I will!” so gently she replied
She watched him leave and then returned to her basket just inside.
She dreamed and purred with happiness, and she could hardly wait
For tomorrow’s assignation with her very special date.

The Garden Shed

The garden shed its wrinkled leaves
As Autumn came at last,
Then petals fell and twigs as well
Doomed by the icy blast.
But soon in Spring just everything
Will bloom again and smile,
We simply have to quietly wait
For just a little while.

A Twisted Yarn

This is a mariner's ancient rhyme
Which tells how, once upon a time,
An Awful Happening filled with dread
A stupid sailor boy called Ned.
'Twas in the days of pitch and pine,
Pirates, and the Onedin Line,
When sailing ships were all you saw
And steam what you let off ashore.
It was aboard the steamer Koko
Trading 'twixt Hull and the Orinoco,
The look-out (Ned) on his lofty perch,
Was fed up with his fruitless search,
Looking at nothing since ten past three
But miles and miles of empty sea.
At last from the crow's nest came a cry
"Caw" said Ned, "A boat I spy!"
(He should have shouted "Ship ahoy!"
But he was, as I said, a stupid boy.)
The crew came hurtling up on deck –
(Yes, one fell down and broke his neck)
They rushed towards the starboard side
To see what Neddy had espied.
Two hundred men leaned out...Oh! Shocks!
The sea poured in all over their socks!
Well, sailors with leanings should desist-
The Koko had got a little list.........
"To port! To port!" directed Ned,
So the crew rushed down to the bar instead.
The Captain staggered on the scene,
Pyjamas (striped), complexion (green).
Sick as an old seadog was he
With every wave that churned the sea.
'Twas said he hated the nautical life,
But not half as much as he hated his wife.
"Cor stone the crows! What an awful rumpus!
You've made me break the lead in my compass!

What ‘orrible thing have you seen, you rogue?”
He shouted at Ned, in his Irish brogue (?)
“I’m ever so sorry, Captain dear,
Just look at that clipper over there!”
The Captain looked – “Give YOU a clip –
That’s a yacht – and it’s going to ram our ship!
Get out of the way!” But down it bore
And rammed ‘em amidships about half past four.
The Captain fumed “It’s all your fault –
Get down there, Ned, and prove your salt!”
“Ta very much!” poor Ned replied
As he carefully scrambled over the side,
Down the ladder and onto the yacht.....
Where he tripped right over a granny knot.
“Well, what’s the damage?” the Captain roared.
“I’ve bumped my shin and I’ve been floored.”
“You stupid nit! Now tie her to,
Then go below and find the crew.”
So Ned complied, and limped around
But not a soul was to be found.
Then in the galley he discovered
Two tasty dishes in the cupboard.
Such lovely girls! who whooped with glee....
They brought him round with cups of tea.
“Hullo, sailor! You look shaken.
You’re just in time for eggs and bacon.”
They told him as the bacon curled
Of their daring voyage around the world.
Two years they’d sailed, and just for larks,
And seen no men at all, just sharks.
Ned had to interrupt by stating
That he couldn’t keep his Captain waiting.
He invited both the girls aboard –
An idea which they just adored!
So up on deck they went and climbed
The ladder, Neddy close behind.
“Cor stone the crows” What ‘ave we ‘ere?
Welcome aboard, my pretty dear!
There’s TWO of you? What lovely charmers!”
(He’s quite forgotten his striped pyjamas!)
Ned followed fast as he could cope

But in his hurry loosed the rope...
(That Ned was daft this tale does prove,
But in fact it was a clever move.)
At last the girls said they must leave,
It had been fun! But who'd believe,
Their darling boat had utterly gorn!
They WERE upset, and so forlorn.
They looked and looked, but on every quarter
There was nothing to see but salty water.
"Dear, dear" said the Captain, "Do not fuss!
Pray continue your journey along of us!"
Of course they all had a marvellous time –
And I've almost come to the end of this rhyme.
But in case you're wondering what became
Of that empty boat – now, what was its name?
With its meal prepared.....I believe you've guessed!
Of course – it was the Marie Celeste.

ND - #0266 - 080726 - C4 - 234/156/7 - PB - 9781784561055 - Gloss Lamination